D1026539

Deborah Keenan

HOUSEHOLD WOUNDS

"Biblical Reference"

Best poems

"How Will I Know When The War is Over?"
"Why Men Are Not Enough"
"Sunday Sch for Brendan"

Parts of "July 27, 1979" (One stanza tr
much of Ginsberg - the root
very good)

"A Poem of Wh Flowers" — like Henry Reed
Very good stanzas: Two hundred of them
came home
while pieces of them are
not missing

Personally I eat up reunion
scenes

Minnesota Voices Project #1

Deborah Keenan (612) 224-6292

HOUSEHOLD WOUNDS

Drawings by Gaylord Schanilec

New Rivers Press 1981

Copyright© 1981 by Deborah Keenan
Library of Congress Catalog Card Number: 81-80547
ISBN: 0-89823-022-5
Book Design: C. W. Truesdale
Typesetting: Peregrine Cold Type

Some of the poems in *Household Wounds* have previously
appeared in the following publications: *Bellingham House
Review*, *Born Again Beef*, *Cottonwood Review*, *Dacotah Territory*,
East River Review National Anthology of Anti-War Poems, *Great
River Review*, *Greensboro Review*, *Poetry Northwest*, *Seems*, *Sole
Proprietor*, and *Wind Literary Journal*. Our thanks to the editors of
these publications for permission to reprint here.

New Rivers Press Books are distributed by
        Small Press Distribution, Inc.
        Jeanetta Jones Miller
        1784 Shattuck Ave.
        Berkeley, CA 94709
Books published in the Minnesota Voices Project are also
distributed regionally by
        Bookslinger
        2163 Ford Parkway
        St. Paul, MN 55116

Household Wounds has been manufactured in the United States of
America for New Rivers Press, Inc. (C. W. Truesdale,
editor/publisher), 1602 Selby Ave., St. Paul, MN 55104 in a first
edition of 1,000 copies of which 20 have been signed and numbered
by Deborah Keenan and Gaylord Schanilec.

SECTION I
PURSUIT

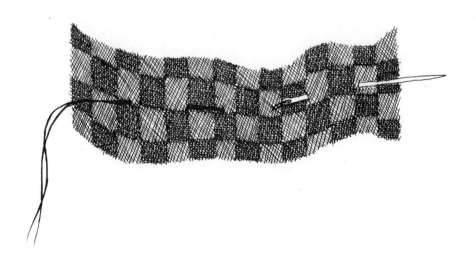

The Drive

The drive toward love
measures itself in the slant of winter
sun breaking on the city left behind,
curving on the bodies of hills.

And the drive toward love is written down
on maps that do not mislead; the map that names
the easiest part: signs, roads, what can be seen.

The car holds its course as I hold mine,
allows no mistakes.
I am the heart inside metal,
the hands that grip the circle,
I am a face in a small mirror,
looking backwards for safety,
looking forward to the "X", the barely decipherable
"me" that lives on the map.

The drive toward love is no myth
though I felt the weight of a story already written,
no new ending requested;
though I felt the row of pines might circle
my car, force me back,
their needles threading the air with the winter word,
intruder.

In the drive toward love nothing is
safe: not the calculated miles of a changeable landscape,
not the words of his voice, "always head north or west",
not the words of passion written down,
memorized like litany,
not even the love traveling the hidden bloodstreams
in all the trails of my body,
all that blood
moving without question,
without hesitation,
toward my heart.

The Recluse

snapped in two like a brittle pencil
like a fresh bean
she lives in a state
barely useful she does not tamper with herself
left on her own for a few free hours
she does not cause trouble does not bite
does not do anything about
ads she reads are not clipped or filed
whether dealing with new life or new casseroles
she cannot do it she does not have affairs
does not read
books for a first time always re-reading
old words but she does not memorize
she does not want it that certain

she has never been able to
she does not see people
does not draw conclusions connections
she cannot do crossword puzzles
she finds things puzzling
veins in leaves pinecones only at the top
of certain trees
she loses her purse her mind her baby's pacifier
her tennis shoes in december
her geraniums are dying but
she knows the image has been used before
some hot-house poet always beating her
to the punch

she reads campaign literature that arrives
secretly under her locked door
she casts a vote and lost thinking suddenly of
the privilege of a secret ballot she cannot remember
how to open the curtain she thinks of buying a voting booth
and making her home inside except she knows
it will be misrepresented misread
too mystifying

she knows it is november
she feels certain some planet is blocking her
claustrophobic she chooses to rest in small rooms
anyway
big rooms demand so much
filling

Whale Sounds At 9:30 A.M.

The orchestra is tuning up.
If they make it through the water
they will perform as announced.
Fewer and fewer bubbles break the surface.
I am afraid for the oboe player. She may not survive.

Some terrible deaths are happening.
One low voice, surrounded by moans, is angry.
He is not strong enough to convince anyone but himself
that it is worth fighting.
Too many of them are crying now.

Some of the musicians have been carried to the shore.
The tide has learned to be hard.
The instruments are on the shoreline filled with salt water
and small fish who cannot believe their lives are ending
inside tubas and clarinets.
They had been unable to resist the lovely brass,
the hand-hammered shell keys.

Two violinists are calling to each other.
They have been in love but have not spoken until now.
I want them to find their ways through the dense waterfall.
I want them to fall into each other's arms.
I want them to admit their passion and find escape.

The helpless moaning and calling does not cease.
I wish they would all die now.
Like the voices of sirens their sobs are enchanting me.

I am above surface now,
but the fourth wave wants to pull me under.
I cannot resist the musicians anymore.
Their lonely shapes, half covered with seaweed,
drift toward me.
They need what is left of my breath
to continue their concert.

Marrying The Fans

There are so many women here tonight.
I have climbed with my summer lover to the second deck,
have found my place in the grandstand, have gotten
dizzy: smells of spilled beer, cigarettes, the stadium
makes me delirious and I pause to reclaim my balance
and notice all these women dressed in white, summer women
who shed their winter disguise and undress
to capture anonymous eyes of men who whoo and screech
in their male preen and ritual.
When I can see more clearly I know these women
are not all in white; sky blue their second choice,
tangerine third; these women are a captured tribe,
some species domesticated by their sex, by their mothers'
secret messages.
I am diminished by every woman I notice. The one in danskins,
the one in a halter top, the one the men bow down to, her face
a smear of conquest. These women frighten me. I am a woman
who has loved women always, never broke a date with a woman
when the man of January or the man of July came calling.
"I know all that," I say to the bleachers. Who raised
these other women? The teasers, the shy ones, carried in
treacherous currents by the more popular, here the sad ones,
too willing to endure for just a touch, a look, free beer, joy-
ride. Here the married ones, abiding their husbands'
scavenger stares, here the old ones, falling from the
Victorian era in dizzying descent, scandalized
by near nakedness and sexual curses that float in grandstand air.
There are so many women here tonight.
They are all dressed in white. They are all being confirmed,
being baptized, they are marrying the fans,
they are so white, their summer skin carries a scent,
sends a message, they are in white.
Impure, they haven't got a prayer that will lift them
from the hungry grandstand to a safe cross.

Sunday School For Brendan

*"My friend says he knows a
secret tunnel to Jesus. He says he can't
take me through because you don't send
me to Sunday school."*

So on an icy sunday morning,
guilt pumping like blood through my mother veins,
we pick a church.
"This one looks holy, mom."
He enters a small room with his list
of questions: where is hell,
why can't I sit in the throne next to Jesus,
where is the tunnel?

I sit through a sermon,
ritual combination: transactional analysis,
hell and brimstone.
I wait at the door for my son
to emerge unscathed from his collision
with faith.

He runs to me, a red paper apple
in his hand on which rests, glued,
a construction paper worm eating its way out,
in his other hand a small white box.

"They didn't want to talk about God and Jesus."
"What did you do?"
"We made houses for things.
Do you see the ghost I made?"

Out of the white box rises
a small opaque shape, crayon marked eyes,
sweet smile drawn by a five year old boy
who believes in ghosts,
who believes in homes for worms and ghosts.

I am cautious, unwilling to tamper
with any small god fever.

"Next week, mom, I think we should go sledding.
Don't you?"
"If you want to."

We leave the house of the biggest ghost,
the spirit of jesus stays behind
to haunt those in the church darkened hallways.

We walk through a tunnel of light,
through white snow.
His red mittens look like hearts.
His small ghost smiles inside the white box.

Biblical Reference

The gideon bible waits restlessly inside
the empty drawer.
The new voices in the room speak of the key
in the lock, of rebirth,
of epiphany, the wine and the blood.

The bible assumes he will be opened soon
by their warm hands seeking his tightly held
wisdom unread since birth.

His longing for the right people to enter
the anonymous room has made him hungry.

He wants his fresh pages to be caressed,
he wants fingers moving everywhere on him,
he wants palms holding him,
he wants to be spoken out loud.

He does not know why it takes them so long,
cannot understand why silence has replaced their words;
he has been well trained,
knows he cannot throw himself against
the side of the bureau,
knows if they do not freely choose him
all that he is will mean nothing.

Their silence is broken with sighs, laughter.
He wants to hear their footsteps;
patient Penelope he waits, if he knew
what it meant to weave,
if he had the hands to do,
his tapestry, an aural imagining,
would drape the room,
twelve-twenty-eight.

He can tell from their voices the couple
is drifting from him, he knows he has misread
the religious quality in the tones of their harmony.

He sinks into reverie: the beige walls seen
as he was carried in, the careless hands
dropping him,
the drawer closing,
the light gone.

Where is the therapist who can cure
him of this terrible claustrophobia?
Where is the mate to help him through
endless dark seasons?

The bible waits for justice,
yearns for mercy, opens himself to the book of Job
to steady himself

while the voices in the room
celebrate
the song of Solomon.

The Cabin In Winter

For Charlie Baxter

The cabin in winter
is deserted and sags under snow.
The bears walk past carrying their picnic baskets.
Dark edges of fish caught in November's freeze
glint like knives through lake's ice.

The nameless lake rests, indifferent.
Her frozen water has no sense of fellowship
with the fish who board under her ice.

The woman who lives in the lake does not cook stews
to warm her inhabitants.
Those who do not remember to sign the register
she flings from the lake.
Moose and deer graze on their aired bodies.

The woman cares only to watch the cabin.
She studies the frame for signs of exhaustion.
She worries over each season's weathering.
She rates the summer visitors, score sheets in hand.
Do they sweep regularly? Wash the windows?
When they clean the fireplace are the ashes buried
or sent to the bottom of her lake?

When couples go naked in spring sun
does the cabin reach to drive splinters into them?
Whom does the cabin tolerate?

She worries over the questions.
She does not care to rise to the surface. She has plans.
She will not forfeit her solitude to mystify any visitor.
She is tempted to cut the dock loose, sink the row boat,
carve messages in the canoe, but she cannot give
up her major plan.

She keeps her files locked in cabinets
lowered and anchored at great cost.
At night she pulls his files, studies his charts,
reads over his dreams she recorded in shorthand
from nights he walked the shore in restless sleep.

She is ready. He will arrive in early spring
for the final visit.
He will clean the cabin.
He has always scored high in general maintenance.
He will walk the beach, and, though tempted,
she will wait for the time
he decides to dive and swim at night.

She locks her files for the time, waiting.
She does not lose her patience.

Watching the bears eat dinner on the balcony of the cabin
she feels jealous of their red wine and checkered tablecloth.
The homely picture moves her to tears.

Pursuit

After she is lured from safety the scene begins.
We do not see what has enticed her, why she wants
it enough to risk the slow movement from the dark
into broken patterns of sunlight on the forest floor.

Fur settled on her skin, eyes without panic,
no sign of a heartbeat out of control.
A normal wild scene; these trees, this sunlight,
roots, weeds, other creatures, the stream.

And she is a part of all this. Not one of us
who sees her can remember we have never seen
her. Now she begins to run; this too looks
right. She, lithe, smooth to touch,

bright eyes running, looks right running
and no one wants to stop her. No.
So she runs. The scene, suddenly ominous, certain
trees too large and sparse, undergrowth tangled,

a harsher green. The stream distended,
over-running its banks. She runs faster now,
pursued by what we cannot see, cannot guess.
We have watched her too long now,

and harmless, easy on the eyes, she compels
our attention; we care how her story ends.
She cares too, and with no break in her stride
she races out of sight, into a darker

region of the forest where our eyes cannot focus,
cannot find her, where our feet do not take us.
And because there is only so much we can give, we turn
our care for her into metaphor, and gracelessly walk away.

History

Virgin Mary protects her own kind.
I lost her years ago.
All the characters have been re-written:
Judas a hero, Peter was in on the plot,
the cock crowing a paid extra;
Mary and Martha, Martha a villain,
unfair, unfair when she worked so
bloody hard to keep order,
all Mary had to do was sit at his feet
and pretend to listen.

Mother Mary does not hold out a hand
to guide me
and the son of god burning in holy fire
the night before
is merely a fevered image
for times I've waited
through endless garden nights.

And the woman at school says she never
understood the tower of Babel.
What does it signify? Why were the people
wrong to build a tower of words?

I've got no answer lady,
I'm here dying
in the chair next to you,
and nothing holy happens in these hallways.

Easter is gone.
We are only waiting for a break in the weather,
I want the pagan sun burning my skin.

There is no protection
when Judas is a hero
and the whole cast of characters

is looking for a virgin they can trust.

I gave up innocence years ago.
Can't remember what it felt like
to be untouched,
to believe.

Wonder Woman Speaks To The Mole People

Although I took this role on graciously
I must tell you I was the inevitable but
uncharmed natural choice. After so much

tunneling you were bound to find this island
and I cannot help that when you emerged mine
was the face you saw. I wanted to tell you

that a search for dark has consumed me just
as your search for light has controlled you.
And though my mission was 'disturb the dark',

the force we created when dark met light
was circumstantial, compelling, but circumstantial.
I felt the gentle hand lead me to you,

I saw you led by this same hand and the
hand was correct; we were meant to find ourselves thus, on an empty island, nowhere

to turn for solace but each other. But
I know you are truly searching for another,
someone more at ease with light, not still

waiting her turn through the dark, rooted
interiors of this earth. I have watched
you catch your breath with me, I have watched

you throw the idea of us around like a bright
penny, and when the coin catches the sun it
seems a good idea, but ideas often seem

right in sunlight, or in dark and harbored
rooms of love, but when left to themselves
they fade, fade and grow dim, and that hurts.

If it is discovered that this dim light is
what I must follow then I will admit my
mistake, will come back to you and fight

with my golden wrist bands the others who
come to claim you, I will come back to you,
dear and gracious leader of the mole people,

we will then see if the air for growth,
the sun for joy, the dark for love can be
matched between us and the others who fight

for entry into our two separate kingdoms.
Although I must tell you again I took the
role on with deep need, great joy, although

I must speak the truth, this is some kind
of completion, but not the final sort we
both know too well. We will meet again

on the mainland. And we will be glad.

Losses And The Color Of Snow

i

now that I am home again from eight months
hopeless and water-locked away from palm fronds
rattle and hiss now I know the only thing
that matters is snow falling

ii

hymn to white   I can't lift my eyes
because pinecones on the fir are still visible

iii

there is no color test that fairly finds me
my choices   gray wolf   white haze

iv

I cannot reach my friends anymore
the telephone shot from my hands
by a perfect bullet
I wait patiently for my intruder to show
his true colors

v

had a friend with dark curls always dressed in red
since losing her in a poppy field I've forced others
around me to wear gray and white so they will not
slip from my vision

vi

the telephone lines seem to sag now that their connection
with this house is finished   I watch for a gray car
carrying a companion but it never comes

vii

we have the only shed on the block with a porthole
the shed is sinking now in drifts and the face
in the window haunts me

viii

I search for a snow shovel
I know there is only one way to save a sinking ship

ix

when my child wakes he will think it is christmas
my hands will be empty when I reach
to lift him and explain the secrets of snow

The Man Who Knew About Winter

He wondered why she moved through the house singing over and over, "so long, it's been good to know ya." And he wondered why all the poems and stories he'd been collecting for years were disappearing from his notebooks; every time he opened one there were more clean, white pages, more indentations left from paperclips that had done something useful, more erased chapter headings.

He wondered why he knew so many women for the first time in his life, why they were all beautiful, slim like weasels, slim like the fantasy woman he kept hidden in his brain, and why the woman who was right this minute walking past him singing, "so long, it's been good to know ya," was, although quite good looking, solid, tall, certainly not the kind of woman to tremble, reed-like, in a winter storm, was more likely to grab a snow shovel and do the right thing with it. Well, it was winter, and he supposed everything needed a second look, deserved a second or third look, he guessed that was why he was suddenly so introspective, so consumed with doubt; his notebooks, his woman, fed up with women, bugged by the kids, he guessed that winter was why but that made no sense, winter, after all, was his favorite season. Only a month ago he'd sworn never to move; he was going to dig in, he'd told a friend, he was no weakling, he was no sun worshipper, hell, no.

So he listened to this woman in the kitchen singing her old cowpoke song, wondered if she was imagining tumbleweeds, cactus, was seeing lizards move across secret sand, what was she doing? The food was cooking, the children were gone, popular children, invited here and there, sometimes he wondered how she kept it all straight, how in the middle of her song, on any day, she would call out, "It's four-thirty, time to pick up Joe or pick up Sally," or time to do something else so that something else could happen later on, in time. Time after time she surprised him, moving as she did, chanting poems, recipes, songs, phone numbers; he remembered she'd told him once her memory was lousy, but she was a liar. Her memory was frightening.

He wondered why he was happy with all this confusion, with a woman singing in the bedroom, "so long, it's been good to know ya," the sounds of drawers being opened and closed. When he fell asleep he wondered why the woman felt suddenly slim like a weasel, slim like fantasy brides, why she hummed in her sleep, why she was suddenly all the women he knew so well, why spring didn't come sooner, why days ended with such grace, why all his nights were like wrapped presents: dreams, the woman, restful sleep.

He supposed winter did this to him. When he woke up he saw that his notebooks were filled again, there were new chapter headings, written in brown ink, when he woke up the children were home, he remembered their faces as if they had never been gone, he heard the woman singing in the kitchen, a quiet song, but it did not sound like a trail song, did not sound like a going away song, did not sound like a blues song, it sounded correct, like the voice of a woman he used to know, supposed he still knew, sounded like a woman who sang haunted rock and roll songs, who paced the house with an imaginary microphone in her hand. He decided to give her a real microphone for Christmas, for Chanukah. It was still winter, he knew December was real, he knew he made her happy. He didn't understand why, but she kept on not leaving, and that was good enough for him.

This Afternoon

is like another and another and that is
no simile I don't even like this afternoon
but a poem waits to be written
there's the smell of dinner cooking a voice
singing tub water running small daughter
calling orders from her world of water
and the man who sits patiently
cataloguing a life he lived without me
each slide holds this memory or that memory
click and he keeps them organized keeps them
dust free keeps them alive with each
click keeps them coming in order click
this perfect pine tree this perfect sun
set this perfect woman click this life
he left behind to sit with me this poet
woman with dinner cooking and a small
girl bathing and the stereo sending the
message of lost love this woman sitting in a
winter afternoon writing a poem click
about a man click who has so many pictures
from his past whose past is so clear framed
preserved protected the past that won't
stay in the past because he clicks it into
the present tense the past that hovers
the past that becomes the present as he
walks out at four-thirty on this afternoon
to go see the perfect woman who is always
present from his past the perfect woman
click who is not me.

Section II

MENDING

"The music says the music cannot be enough
But anyway some current will pass through deadened arms,
And all the stories will be original again."

from "Cantata At Midnight"
Charles Baxter

omit

Extended Metaphors

They are my present triumvirate.
They speak: she is the sun,
no, the moon,
no,
a star.

They forget me as they battle to define
me. All three pretend to hate war,
all carry their wounds differently, enjoy
presenting their scars; the stitches of their various
doctors give them pleasure. I can see none of them
as astronauts; too bad,
since I am placed in the sky.
At the moment they are brand-new lawyers, over-eager, filled
with facts, their texts more precious than anything
my earthly hands might give.

Sun: I am unhurried, daytime steady, constant,
I burn out so slowly he doesn't worry about losing
me. I last, grant new life,
am not selective when I give warmth.

Moon: I control tides, I am the secret,
I am cyclical, I am rose blood monthly, I should be
dark haired but he forgives me, blonde will do for now,
I am the cause of tidal waves, beautiful in my coming,
awesome then forgotten
in the terrible rebuilding of his landscape.
I disappear, slipper small, luminous only in memory,
I haunt, bear mysteries, not children.

Star: I am some light. I do not fit
into constellations already plotted,
I burn only myself, I light emptiness pointlessly,
I am already gone when he sees my shining,
I plummet, fall endlessly,
my long descent delights him.

He says, "Oh look, a falling star."
and kisses his new lover,
while I do my meteoric dive,
while I am dying,
all the while hoping I break
open, burn out, turn to hard, black rock
inside ocean.
I do not want to die on land.

What they have done to me
no longer is a question worth answering.
I know I can no longer bear
being personified by any
one but myself.

I am the tree, no, not that one,
I am here, smaller than any star,
I am rooted, though I understand why I forget
that truth sometimes; I travel long distances
for lost water sources.

In the winter I am so filled with death
even I forget I live.

I have not been done in by some reckless bonsai gardener.
I am not an easy species.

I cause no natural disasters
except my own.

Next year, after I receive spring's fair gift,
I plan to become a woman.
We'll all see what will come of that
metaphor.

The Path Of The Hands

(handwritten annotation: echoes Robert's hands (small) cage)

i

fingers play games
fingers are frightened mice
are clever spiders
are little men running from
certain doom
are marchers in parades for the deaf
fingers move over carpet
silently the children are
enchanted   the fingers
come home to their owner
and sleep in palms
and children sleep
and fingers dream
of children touching them

ii

her hands take the shape
of a miniature temple
no nursery rhyme
but a true place of worship
and a chorus of trained
voices emerges from the
stained glass fingers
and echoes through the walls
of her hands the temple
and she tightens her hands
into fists and there is
no more song

iii

hands lay on her stomach
each finger a bar of a small
precise birdcage   the cage
closing at the top with
two fingertips like nails
going into each other

this small boned birdcage
waited   waited for the right
bird to fly in but the
right bird never came
and the woman whose
hands they were
died and grew
wings

The Sorceress

Funny but... provincial

i
The sorceress returns from another hard day,
too tired to clean the castle,
practice her mail-order chants, mix potions,
change anyone's life for the better.

She needs her eight hours.
Since her return from the sea she has not dreamed.

The tape recorder attached to her telephone
is always filled with sobbing voices.
Mothers-in-law, randy, straying husbands,
children gone bad,
the petty needs of the people wear her to a frazzle.

She has never learned to say no with any authority.
Her successes are legendary, but her castle is a mess.

ii
Her jester's toes have forgotten how to dance.
His bells are rusting.
He cannot juggle anymore.
He sits in the kitchen, trying to recover
his lost art, but the apples roll on the floor.
The cook is fed up. She wants only a floor safe to walk on.

The jester believes he can no longer amuse the sorceress.
His mother's words haunt him,
"Yes, but can you make a living at it?"

iii
The sorceress walks through town.
Children, no longer crippled, play kick-the-can.
They do not recognize her.
Grateful mothers trail her,
pressing fresh vegetables into her hands.
The sorceress tries to decline.
She has no appetite.

The sorceress retreats into the forest, carrying her burdens.
No one follows.
The villagers believe the forest is where she does
her best work.
It is not.
She goes there only to gather wildflowers.
She presses them between sheets of waxed paper
during sleepless nights.

iv

A red-haired sailor is waiting for her
when she returns from the woods.
He tries to crowd her.
She cannot believe he has misunderstood.
Has he never heard of shipboard romances?

He believes in his charm.
He believes his body has cast an unbreakable spell on hers.

She knocks him into the moat, crosses over,
orders the guards to lift the drawbridge.
She assumes he can swim.

v

The sight of the sailor has helped.
This night, like a doctor unwilling
to be on call, she unplugs her phone.

She uses her gift,
creating a wine to drink for dreaming.
She goes to sleep knowing
her night will be rich with tangled plots,
unsought images, the colors of the sea,
the boat, lost in fog.

In her body's final turning before dawn,
the face, luminous, of her loss,
hovers behind her closed eyelids.

When she wakes, her heartbeat has slowed
to a more human rate.

She rings for breakfast.
The cook's eyes fill.
"I believe the crisis has passed once more.
If she asks to see the children,
things may get back to normal around here."

vi
Music fills every turret.
The jester opens up the main ballroom and begins
brushing up on his tap dancing.
The sorceress and her children are laughing
in the nursery.
The phone rings incessantly.
The callers cannot contain themselves,
begin to speak before the beep.

vii
The sorceress knows the fever has passed.
Her hands are not shaking, her children's eyes
neither give nor reflect any unhealthy sorrow.

She has known for years that surviving
is her greatest talent.
The rest has always flowed
from the acquired magic.

Stainless Steel

Service for eight, paid for with deposit,
my bank woos me
and I fall
in love with the idea of steel
without stain.

My bank does tricks, (corningware tricks, amfm radio tricks,
luggage, blanket tricks) to get at my money.
They take my money with sleight of hand
and pull loans, cars, mortgage payments
from the black hat that waits in their vault.
They play with my money.
I play with their almost free cutlery.

I play to win.
I steel myself against losing the game
to some more clever word god.

And, I play with the actual forks,
liking the implications (What can three steel points control?)
I like the spoons' hollows,
I like the direct message of the knives.
I like all the cold steel slipping through
my hands.
I like seeing the box that holds, hides
the stainless steel.
Printed there in small letters: pattern—freedom.

Even freedom is a pattern,
and I've got service for eight.
My secular longings slice open the poem.

I must find seven other people to sit down with freely.
I must go now to search for the pattern
implied in freedom.

I must go now to put away my stainless steel
and hide the knives somewhere
I cannot easily discover
until the implications
vanish
and finally I can sit down to eat.

The Woman Who Knew About Winter

Times her heart beat normally, brain waves scanned to the rhythm of a waltz, ah, Vienna, those times more than others she knew winter was the reason, the cause, the answer, the question.

True, sometimes she thought winter was only the cause, usually she knew better, but now that the snow was sifting through the windows, now that the cats had left town, their knowledge of migration patterns a mystery and misery to her bird-loving friends, now she wondered.

Her children polished their skate blades, sang winter songs on key, her daughter particularly caught by the phrase, "Three turtle ducks and a park in a pear tree," her son particularly caught by his sister's ignorance of song lyrics. They were busy, had their own lives already and the oldest was only six. So, she would wander away from their lyrical disagreements, leave them in the echo of their words, a last refrain of "Santa claus is coming to town" ringing in her ears. She would go to her bedroom, haven from the real world; sometimes the woman worried about calling her bedroom a haven, worried about the implications, what did she think constituted the real world, anyway? She could remember with very little effort the loving, the gentle words, certain details of the man's hands, she knew those things were part of the real world, so why did she, when alone, hesitate, call those things, by implication, an illusion?

There was no answer. Or: there was an answer, no doubt hidden inside rock and roll lyrics, but lately she had been unable to turn the channel selector away from the classical station. And what did that mean, she asked, having gotten out from under the last question. What did it mean to suddenly be choosing to play music with no words? She was not a snob; even though she played classical music she always referred to it as music with no words, as if the words were the things to be valued. She didn't want anyone thinking she knew the names of concertos, knew any of the numbers or flats or sharps that composers assigned to their noted genius. She knew *The Pastoral Symphony* and *The Mouldau*, the latter because her college roommate was a Smetana junkie, had to

44

listen to *The Mouldau* once a day or she couldn't deal with the pressure of undergraduate life. The point was that whenever the woman heard classical music she liked, if she was with someone else, she always asked, "Isn't that *The Pastoral Symphony*? No, I mean, *The Mouldau*?", and of course it wasn't either of them, though she had honestly thought it could have been.

She supposed that those two memorized titles indicated that she wanted secretly to live in the country by a river. But that couldn't be since she not secretly at all wanted to live by the Atlantic ocean near a city with forty movie theaters, in a climate without snow, but which possessed bracing winds, occasional stunning storms, and well, perhaps snow that fell once in ten years, or once in a hundred, as it did in Florence and Rome.

The woman realized in the time it had taken to explain this much she had arrived back to the idea of winter, back to the actual word snow. No, actually, since this was no word game, back to the actual snow that was no longer sifting but was instead piling up in her room.

And, although the woman generally loved to think about what was hidden inside, or buried underneath other things, snow held out no mystery worth solving. It was what it was, and what it was she wanted no more of. She was no regional writer, afraid of permanent writer's block if she changed landscapes. She knew more poems and stories were hiding everywhere: in the everglades, in the jungles, in the empty deserts, were waiting in every town she'd never seen, in every place she'd never walked.

And she came to see that winter was not the cause, or effect, was not the answer or the question. Was not even a symbol since symbols are rarely so cold, rarely turn to slush, rarely invade whole rooms with their real presence. The point was: what could she do with it now that she had it? And, she knew all too well, what she could do with it was live with it or leave. And why she didn't leave was the chapter that was hiding inside the typewriter keys. Unfortunately, the room where she wrote was adrift with sifting piling snow, and the typewriter was buried and the spring thaw was nowhere in sight, although signs of rebirth were everywhere.

She knew enough to seek warmth, but she was not a bird, migration was not a natural talent, and since she hated birds anyway she hadn't used a bird metaphor for years. She was not planning to fly away, just to leave gracefully like a human whose heart beats in three-quarter time should do, when they finally admit winter is no longer their natural element.

City Life

when I was childless
country living was my dark heart's desire
I needed the improbable burnished autumns
the violet trees in october
seen through any country window
I courted the need to be alone and the need
to drown in a lover's hunger
with only a dirt road connecting me
to some aging city I never wanted
to live in anyway

and when I was childless and he had left
walked down the gravel road
away from my country face
then I moved closer
needing the heartbeat of the city
almost imperceptible in my ear
needing vague neon choruses of light
to woo my eyes away from   just trees
just land   just those country colors

and when the children came
and the husband was gone
then I had to have the city's pulse
inside my blood helping my heart
keep the beat   the steady city metronome

saying over and over through city winters
impossibly gray
saying   there are strangers everywhere
they carry secrets they are at your door
just reach to them with those improbable city hands
impossible though it seems to do reach
some hands may reach back although no one knows
your name
they will recognize your city face
they will know why you are here

What Will Last

For Jay Peterson

To say what hurts:
all the why's spread out like cold
butter, wrecking the last piece of bread
in the house.

Who's to say what words
will soothe
if you could only feel them pierce
your mind, precise, painless
arrows.

Who's to say how long
we might last:
longer than the time before at least,
as if we thought we could apply
for any warranty longer than seven years.

Who's to say except you and me;
we rise and fall in this house,
our bodies huddled over jig-saw puzzles.
I lose my sense of what piece fits where,
trying to stop every ordinary activity
from turning relentlessly
into a puzzle I cannot solve.

We rise and fall,
our bodies meet and are put back together,
we are the jig-saw puzzle that works,
fits at least one more time.

Who's to say we might not
survive our own disparate yearnings
each time they emerge.

We face off against our own shadows
longing for high noon
when we can forget
for a moment
that they exist.

The Mother

For Virginia Wells Bowman

your meeting at yellowstone
the mountains were a fact
you did not realize they could be lost through love
so you traveled to him across plains   east
mormon woman   what travesty to head for daybreak's edge
aiming your heart like an arrow at that gray-eyed
presbyterian

home home you said to yourself
the lush flat green of prairie
when did your eyes begin to ache for the rockies
perhaps when he said the names
nakomis   johanna   minnetonka
the lakes of this northern state
no fair exchange for your loss

but did we not play pioneer so adequately
for his gray eyes
dressed in aprons stained with the juice of currants
wild raspberries
we filled the fruit cellar with proof
of love   adaptability

the years of harvest passed
he fell ill   grew oblivious
to your slow rooting
in the flat lands where passion led you

and you grew only stronger
your now midwestern hands are still
holding back the wilderness
and shaping inner forms of children's children

like the mountains you left
you are strong   steady
you endure   like they   the terrible winds
the change of season
you endure time's unceasing movement
through all your landscapes

The Father

For Clifford A. Bowman

three acres
pale moon garden that was my father
lilacs carried in burlap from pennsylvania
for his new home
pine trees planted   now old and scarred
brush fires set by careless children

rosebushes tethered to spikes of oak or birch
the flowers he eased through
late spring snows   grasping grape vines
planted too near
evenings he watched the vines lean and bent them new

this garden   now run and staked by strangers
where my summers passed endless
hoe and rake   my fingers watching his
"you must learn to press the seeds into earth this way"

the horizontal maple
stripped of branches for firewood
the trunk left whole for my sake
barked pony of childhood wishes

now flowerless suckers tear my hands
I do not coax rosebuds from this over-run plot
the grapevine tangles and gives no fruit

only the lilacs endure these winters
this neglect
there are fewer sprigs each spring
no one has ridden my maple horse
and moss and insects rejoice
in their hollowed paradise

Household Wounds

You are cutting apples for your children.
You are committed to their health, and with every bite
they swallow your guilt is appeased,
somewhat, the guilt you feel buying bubble gum,
or the guilt you feel handing out cookies at 4:30,
when you know real food, a proper dinner
will march out of the oven at 5:00.
A digression: you are still cutting
apples, and the knife searches for a truer direction,
and your second finger meets the blade
and red apple blood runs
down the drain.

You are reading bedtime stories. An important
ritual, such a right thing to do
it amazes you. Nights your children would rather
play one more game of octopus eating a submarine
you lose your temper, say sternly, books
or bed, that's your option. You can't help it;
you believe in books, and tonight, reading
Leo the Late Bloomer, you are so happy,
the children lean into your body, their elbows
find spaces of you never before explored,
you reach to turn the page and
your son says, don't cry
as he watches you cry,
a paper cut that sliced
open your third finger,
page five,
more blood.

You are learning to be handy. You want
to build bookcases, repair the furnace, chop
wood and celery, you want to do it
all, and you want to do it all
right. Your therapist warns you

51

every week, you can't do it
all. Well, you know that. You hold up
your hands in surrender; the smashed thumb
awarded by the hammer, the airplane you built your son
has flown away, your thumb reminds you
of your accomplishment.
The two fingers wrapped in band-aid sheer strips,
the angry burn that hides in your palm,
you touch it and remember cooking your first
batch of spaghetti, you touch it
and remember how you forgot
to use hot pan holders.

No one can see the symmetrical line of bruises
that linger on your left leg; you, falling off steps,
you, shovelling the snow that won't stop
falling, just like you won't stop
falling.

The headache from standing up under the stairwell,
you always forget to remember the potential for harm
in a home; you don't want paranoia
to rule you.

You want: the walls smooth, the steps untreacherous,
you want the ceiling to stay up, the lightbulbs lit,
the linoleum flat, the rugs glued in place,
the toys put away, the cutlery dull, the scissors
hidden, the needles and pins melted down and used
for some vital part of an airplane that will take you
away from all this
danger.

Mending

just to match thread and fabric
takes a year

a needle sharp enough
an eye big enough to pass through
to see clearly from
exactly what it is that needs mending

just to match the torn place
with a patch
that will not call attention to itself
takes more than years

just to find what's been torn
and what's worth mending
seems like years go by

and my hands are not graceful
or kind about this task
they dial my mother's number
they speak with my voice over the wires
mother they say will you mend this
will you mend this too

and though she agrees
as I knew she would
there's so much mending to be done
and what has been torn
will take years to mend
and I cannot ask her for that much
time

it's my turn to mend
and I won't tell anyone
how long it might take

After

i
you've seen a three foot long
white cat watching you from a fence
in Scotland there's not much left.
No one believes you anyway;
you put amazement away in a junk drawer
of feelings you no longer harbor.

ii
After you've had the babies,
have screamed with the slash of new life,
well, then, all the pain your men feel
with their cut fingers, aching stomachs,
spring colds, it leaves you cold.
No sympathy, ice heart, you don't care.
Want to scream: get off your back,
go to work, you don't know, you don't know.
They call that narcissism.
Women I know well suffer that dread disease.

iii
After you've lost your best friend
to an insatiable cancer that consumed her,
well then, other conversations seem
inconsequential. No energy for small talk,
big talk. She's just dead. Burned to ash
wearing the pink nightgown you gave her;
you don't bother going to the grave,
she's not there anyway, still inside
putting pressure on your heart, appearing
in alternate frames of a Japanese movie,
hiding in the way some women have of holding
china teacups.
Stopping you in the middle of love-making,
slight smile: do it for both of us she says.

iv

After you're not so young anymore.
Too much behind you to feel new, not much
to do with the dizzy feeling of being
your own stranger in a place you name home
for lack of more accurate words. After you
pace and play Salt Lake solitaire until your
hands bleed with the shuffle, after you throw
all the photo albums out the window, after all
this you find out it's only ten in the morning
and the sun is leaving again, just like always.

v

After all this time you can't quite figure out what keeps you
here besides the kids, the poem, the smell of lilac invading
your room, as your friend without wings does a slow dive
outside your window and you can't even catch the hand she
offers you in her grace-filled descent. After all this time.

Steps To Follow For Writing A Happy Poem

Get a mother who wants one.
Have her tell you over and over;
this repeated desire on her part
will help build momentum
for writing what is called a happy poem.

Get to traveling in the past
where supposed happy memories linger.
Grab those memories with your cold fingers,
with your teeth,
any tool for holding will do, will have to
do, then try to start
your happy poem.

So you failed, well then, move
in the future.
America's a nation of future trippers,
you can become one too, inspite of your therapist's
warnings; so seduce, then ravage
your fantasies,
try to sleep several dream cycles in a row,
(if you have small children move to the next stanza)
then begin to write your happy poem.

Try not to make it sound too much
like science fiction.
Your mother is not stupid.

Find yourself a drink that comforts;
apple cider, fresh pressed in the countryside
where you always think you want to live,
scotch, some new drink not connected
with past drinking, past lovers,
old rituals of swallowing.

Eat something never before eaten,
a soft-boiled egg, your passport,
make something edible
and explore the inside of your mouth.
Then write that happy poem.

Avoid, at all costs, the present
tense. Do not write a poem which contains winter.
Do not use the words: loss, burial, mourning;
words like those weigh too much, perhaps
you should wait until spring
to try this.

Go now, easily, away from your typewriter.

Comfort your mother, she deserves it,
let her know happy poems
are just around all your metaphorical corners,
let her know when they come
you will dedicate them to her,
go, cheer the woman up,
she's been through enough
with you, whatever your age might be.

Why We Live In St. Paul

For Jim and Trish

Because we need to forget every day where
we live and by living here
we accomplish that.

Because when we tell people we live
in Minneapolis we know it is a mistake,
not a lie.

There is no Minneapolis, no freeway
crossing the Mississippi river
so that we can arrive

night after night in what pretends to be
Minneapolis but which is really just
movie theater after movie theater

where we hide, longing for a double feature
that will so diminish our city that we
will never have to go home to it, wherever it is.

Because we need a place like this,
which is no place,
we need St. Paul because neighborhoods

here don't match and by straying from one
to the other we forget we have a home
just down the block, just up the street.

Because we need a place to keep our
shell collection, a place to empty our pockets
of quarters and used movie tickets,

because we need steps to walk up,
the quiet pause, the waiting to see if the key
fits the lock.

We need all this, we need
to wonder if we have a place to come home to,
and every day, every night, we arrive,

we say: this is why we live in St. Paul,
because it is a holy, unknown place,
where no one wants to live, where we can barely find ourselves.

Section III

HOW I WILL KNOW
WHEN THE WAR IS OVER

My Hands At Seven P.M.

The last caress has been given.
My hands are not ready to hold a cigarette,
not ready to crochet, not ready to wash up.
My hands want to be on my mind. And they are.
Resting there. My hands will not go away this week.

My hands want to picket winter.
I do not allow them to,
so they crack the skin that holds them.
They want to be martyrs
so they bleed silently into the pattern of the sheets.

My hands are restless on the arms of my chair.
They are restless on my arms.
They have given so much comfort today
they are feeling suddenly useless.
My hands have never learned to fall in love
with each other.
They have learned to chart the heat waves
in my children's foreheads.
My hands could learn the hot and cold of all children.
I am afraid my hands will not be kind to each other
in their old age.

My hands are speaking to me with harsh, angry words.
They are telling me their lost dreams of dancing,
kabuki style.
They are making nasty remarks about Marcel Marceau.
They are telling me they want all the applause.
They are telling me people would not laugh at them
if I were Italian.
They are telling me what and who they will not touch.
They are reading revolutionary literature.
They take turns turning the pages.

My hands are not sure of anything this week.
My hands would make the deaf weep and laugh this week.
My hands have been letting go of china for days.
My hands have a passion for children this week.
They refuse to touch anything less important.

My hands refuse to sleep.
They weave the air and blankets all night.
My hands are too sad to dream.
They have forgotten how to sleep
and only know when to begin again.

What It Is

springs from this deep hollow
like the space air fills
under the bird's arcing motion.

This emptied feeling,
china cup that will never be filled.

Spring air and I falter
in the blue, in the warm,
this sound that can find

no voice in free air.
Deep hollow echoes nothing
but loss, loss, I want

to frame it,
I want to cage it,
walls of blood,

luminous it should shine
to disturb the dark
with the message of emptiness.

Dark stone descending,
endless fall,
well with one wish left;

I am leaving
this age, I am leaving
the children whose birthdays I celebrate.

Where the sound of new life disappears,
that's where I go,

dark hollow I join you.
We will grow
again together,

deep blood, smooth stone,
married we emerge in a colder time.

Must I take care of you
this whole lifetime left?
What is cherished here?

White Orchids

In Memory of Larry Adelman

white orchids
flown in by pat nixon
faithful wives
whose breasts have not been touched
for seven years
suddenly their bodies
smell of exotic flowers

they buy new dresses
stop eating
nationwide we sit
and hear a husband ask
"are you fat?"
"no" she says pleased
with herself

they call that question
a reaffirmation of normalcy

a never ending tape
of men marching from airplane steps
saluting

god bless america

nixon says they have made it all worthwhile
two hundred come home
whole pieces of them are not
missing

personally I eat up reunion scenes
but as the today show flickers
in early morning
I watch and fill with rage
I think of a friend
who came home from the war
at a bad time for good p.r.

he stays with us
when he comes to the veteran's hospital
to have another artificial leg made

I think of his drinking his violence
the way he holds my son gently
I think of white orchids
and the smell makes me sick

The Subject

In Memory Of Wendy Parrish
Dear Friend 1950-1977

i
We will paint this picture now,
the only one worth painting, at once
compelling, inviting,
an essential background, blue sky,
sun, of course, heat should shimmer
off the canvas.
We are doing well, novices no longer,
add some trees, for shade, for beauty,
then the water, moved by imperceptible wind,
this is our canvas, not mine alone,
so the wind must be controlled.

The canvas has been stretched, now must stretch more
to include brown and gold children.
The child with daylight hair, the child
whose hair carries the reminder of autumn.
These children are moving
on the canvas, they move for too many reasons
to list, just to let them move, on or off
the canvas; they help carry the picture's
true message.

Off to one side the mother rests, her face turned
to sun; let it be seen in this painting
that she is willing it all to continue.
Let it be understood: she can be motionless
because the other guards
these painted children.
The mother's face should be at once fierce and peaceful.
A hard face to capture.

The canvas expands, we artists cannot stop
the images we collect, the canvas
can bear all these scenes, collected in so many

pairs of eyes, the canvas wants to contain
all that is remembered.

ii
The central figure in this painting
is moving at the water's edge
in lilac, in navy blue, and the temptation
is strong in me, I want to add the wind
that will move her hair, that will push her scowling
back to me, saying, "Hell, this wind. I don't know why
you enjoy it so much."
I want my answer included on the canvas. "Look,
we share this disagreement, and few others. Go ahead,
call the children, then help me
pack up this clutter, all right, call the children.
We will go home. The wind in the city will be kinder."

iii
The canvas will not dry. God knows I have placed
it in cool rooms, hot rooms, have placed it against
trees in winter wind, in spring sun, but the paint
will not dry, it shines, the canvas is not full,
wants more,
we artists have worked hard, and although we have succeeded
in some ways,
        that background,
        the children,
        these women,
there is so much more the canvas
hungers for, and there is not one among us
who would not have chosen, give the chance,
to have image after vision after image
collect, always there would have been
too much to paint, so much we would have put
our brushes down with relief, let ourselves
fall into this constantly incomplete canvas.

iv

We will paint this picure now,
the only one worth painting.
No gallery can deny us as we move relentlessly
into another summer.
    The sun,
    the children,
    the mother,
alone now, alert to their every motion.
She will not turn her face to the sun as often
this season,

and on some other canvas her face will be
shadowed, eyes liquid,
some essential sorrow painted there
that no brush strokes away.

Arbitrary Winter

i
The precise Rousseau jungle arrives in the mail.
Why can't my friends understand they upset the balance
I struggle for daily with their careless act?
Life in the tropics is hard enough;
my apartment, overwhelmed, gives in:
sprouts, blooms, harvests itself. I grab the last
untangled vine, swing out the window,
an almost fatal escape.

ii
Am I free to live anywhere?
I head for a colder climate.
I need an arbitrary winter season
so that nothing gets out of hand.

iii
Resettling burdens me.
My polite domestic potted plants keep choosing
to live without my help.
My time is consumed; endless shopping for overcoats,
boots, I replace each lost pair of mittens,
spend the rest of my time wondering
why I lose them so carefully,
week by winter week.

iv
Geese fly north over my house.
Their celebratory "v"
darkens the sky.
The thaw is unstoppable, the streets flood.
I am carried away by April water.
I try to convince myself it was time to move on.

v

Can nothing stop this?
Everywhere I travel summer is.
The roadside fruit and vegetable stands alarm me.
So much has been harvested; it is only July.
The fruit is mythic, carries the circle shape
to extremes.
I have to buy something so I won't die
but feel trapped in some allegory of bountiful fruition.
I need my daughter stolen from me heartlessly
so that everything will finish for a while and
I can get some sleep, make a plan.

vi

I lie down on a summer field in night air.
The northern lights, the moon arcing up from the east,
each flower alive in its own grace;
their messages glow with clarity.
I choose to give up for the first time and fall
asleep: no tears, no strategies, knowing nature
will make all my decisions but the final one.

A Poem About White Flowers

my father chose a train
gave it the gift of his body
bright july sun
the engine lifted his form
hurled it scattered it moved on
we pretended there was enough left
to cremate

and the white flowers you gave me are so right
they fill my home I think of them
slashes of petal white
I play endless game after endless loss
of solitaire
just so I can sit with those slashing white flowers
I love these flowers from you
they surprise me the way the roses didn't
they touch me the way a good white cliché
is supposed to touch all women who believe
in words like white and fragrance who believe
in daisies pretending to be zinnias and in daisies
swearing they are white chrysanthemums

by the tracks my brother searched
for father's property
july sun burning to nothing the last
fragments of my father's beautiful
piano hands
he found the wallet torn pictures
pieces of identity that identified
a man who came to dread his own

by the train station my brother found
two lovers who had been giving each other
their bodies
when they heard the train's emergency scream
they forgot the pleasure they had been seeking
and sought another

when they looked up the air carried
my father toward them they were frightened
by the blood the choice of death
so near their open fields of love

and the white flowers you gave me
don't fade today the white
phosphorescent against a winter gray window
I love them for not fading today
for being white not red not dying not red
for being white and themselves
whatever they are whatever they become

The Only Dream I've Had In Months

Balloons are everywhere.
They are caught in the spires, caught in the belfries;
the bells send them higher with the wind
of their ringing.

My mother's furniture has been placed
carefully on the green turf.
I wonder how the college convinced her to share.

My family and I walk sedately under blue sky.
The carnival is somber on green lawn.
No ferris wheel, my son is weeping.

Then, without warning, they are gone and gray churches
surround me. I cannot see around the corners
and I am suddenly cold.

I see a friend sitting on my mother's velvet couch.
His arm is thrown across the carvings that decorate the back.
He is talking. His happiness radiates.
The sunlight is on him and the churches have withdrawn,
leaving him space enough to be expansive.

I am frightened without my children,
but the man is so close to me
I can feel the comfort he will give.
The words gentle and understanding have always marched
in front of his name.

I do not ask permission as I sit down next to him;
after all, it is my mother's couch.
Somehow he is still cloaked in sunlight,
but I am in shadows.

And I, who at my boldest can barely shake hands
lift his arm that caresses the carvings
and pull it round my shoulders.

Even the clothes he wears seem to pull away from me.
He continues to speak. He continues to laugh.

Does he believe I am just a shadow out to spoil his sunny day?
My face flushes, my hands grow even colder.
He lifts his arm to gesture
and I run.

The baby wakes.
The dream is over.
My ration card is punched.   ·
"No more dreams until May," says my belligerent dream-maker.

"You were lucky to get one."
On the gray autumn day of my real life
I am moved to protest.
"Unfair," I say, "How dare that dream be my dream?"
A rare desire for revenge fires me.
I carefully imagine another carnival
where he will be lost inside some dark, windowless church,
and though I hear his voice call, aching for rescue,
I will walk past and tell my son it is only the ghost
of the tower
having a bad dream.

Unasked For

My son and I visit faceless friends.
They are glad we've come.
They say both our names out loud,
use our names like coins, buy our trust.

They take us to their bedroom where windows overlook
a pretentious inner court.
Tropical plants hunger up the walls.
The fountain magnetizes him.

I invent finger games, love him with my hands
more than usual. I want his skin near me,
but each time we finish he turns away to stare
at the giant, phosphorescent carp moving in the bowl
of the fountain; they know he is enchanted.
Their natural routines would make Esther Williams weep.

The window sill is level with the bed as I visit
and he stares and my friends laugh
at a joke with no dream punchline worth remembering
when morning breaks.

I am nervous but these friends like my friends with faces
have renounced cigarettes and announce the fact
with a child's face on a sign ballooning,
"Thanks for not. . . ."
I am not stupid. My hands play with my son and never reach
for what is hidden in my purse.

I cannot remember why I felt I had to leave the room.
The hardest part of dreaming is getting the motives clear.
But I did walk away from him, away from the window
as if I had a reason.
I did not ask them to watch out for him.
Did I think they would be offended, some spoken accusation
poisoning the air? I don't think I left
for a cigarette; almost any reason
would be good to possess but the dream is relentless,
moves on. I am not allowed any excuse.

I was only just outside the door when I ran back knowing
it was too late.
He was kneeling on the windowsill and they were talking
and I was running through their shag carpet, the strands
of wool had become snowdrifts around my feet.

Because it is a dream he is not smashed or broken, his blood
stays inside his small body.
I reach out my hands to his form.
His body has taken the shape of a swastika on the tile floor.
The fish turn away from the edge of the pool, languid
and soft-boned, they know they can no longer charm him.

I sit up, wondering how I could ever have fallen
asleep again after losing him
from such a great height.

July Twenty-Seventh, Nineteen-Seventy Nine

i
My father's death certificate looks casual.
Some hands on this date eight years ago wrote:
"Direct cause: mangling. Engineer applied breaks.
All reasonable effort made to avoid contact." Well,
there you have it.

ii
When my brother wrote me the letter he said,
"There was nothing left but little pieces."
I cried again, though living in Denmark only one
other person could hear me and he is gone too,
less violently, the loss as incalculable.

iii
The death certificate is white. The print dark blue.
This morning I sat in my usual chair,
my mother talking to me of wills, insurance,
money, the house, talking about facts.
It rained all night, that slow steady kind
that doesn't scare.
As we sat talking the blue, deep blue sky broke
through the gray, like his eyes, my most easily traced
legacy from him.

iv
I keep hidden other gifts passed along.
Inside this eight year old scar I carry the imprint
of bad weather and of a single hot July morning.
That's me: married to heat and bad weather.
Inside the heart I carry serious truths
about ways to die, about ways the cards are dealt,
about the way life goes wrong.
Inside my mind are his poems, written with a pseudonym,
though he was not ashamed of his name or words.

v

Father. I write all my poems with my true name.
Father. I write all my poems so I may bury you more kindly.
Father. I write all my poems to keep you alive.
Father. Your gravestone is too small, horizontal with the earth.

That's not good enough. I will dig it out.
I want the headstone vertical, parallel with trees,
hollyhocks, parallel with my stance as I stare down
at where your small pieces, burned and burned, hide.
I want things parallel now, poem for poem,
gray eyes to gray eyes,
track to track.

Say Good-Bye

saying good-bye
took too much pain
took a hard frost
took a long winter
in two souls
saying good-bye
is like all the rock and roll songs
played top volume in a green and white house
is like no song ever written
is like no poem can ever explain
saying good-bye
was as unnatural as endless summer
was as natural as breathing in
whatever air was needed
saying good-bye
too cruel
impossible not to do
saying good-bye
I want to say
I will never do it again
saying good-bye
I want to say it is my
native language
saying good-bye
good-bye
don't say hello
your voice echoes
in all my empty
space
say good-bye

The Other Lover

leaves his shadow like a calling card
drops ashes in a home with no cigarettes
never calls when the children are near
the other lover
hides in the writing room
falls out of envelopes
hides in your dark bed
when the real lover is gone

he's the words in a book you want to read
is discovered when happy alone
no spoiler   a reminder for now
blade bright   almost painless

he's the bookmark you couldn't throw away
he's the dinner you eat alone
he's the tears that shake your complacency
he's the anger you nourish
he knows what he's doing

the other lover is rarely three dimensional
shadow dark and unexpected
more compelling than summer
he is what you need
a few times a year
he is everything a few times a year

if he were content with his role
you could rest easy
but he refuses to be banished
there is no safety
he feeds   he feeds and grows

no matter how powerful your illusions
he is the stronger more willful conjurer
creates himself again from the dust
of your denial

constantly reborn   infinite disguises
he is the secret you confess
to anyone who will listen
but his effortless transformations
his casual departures make all your priests
think him unimportant   ephemeral

the other lover hides in your second heart
and who are you to think you don't need both
to keep your blood alive and flowing?

Why Men Are Not Enough

today she took the moon as her lover
fit him on like a glove
did it the way her mother taught her
fingering him on and moving through moon cloth
and it was only yesterday she took a fallen star
into her and held its light until it came
true like a blood wish
and it was only last week she was mistress to the river
memorized its ripples and let her dress open
white moon on white river breasts
and then last year she married the wind
and promised to be faithful
to its wild rocking and pulse
but when she was sixteen she swallowed venus
made too many wishes and ruined her chances
for a normal life
and when she was little enough for innocence
she put the earth in a secret place
where her brothers would never look and she wouldn't
give it back to the universe
until suppertime
and when she was that little and innocent
she sat down at the dinner table calm and shut like the april
rose her father cultivated and ate with her family
and even asked for seconds
and they all remarked how much bigger she'd grown
this summer and she didn't say a word.

How I Will Know When The War Is Over

we are all assigned wars
we are all assigned friends who die
in war   during years of private war
we are all assigned men to love who burn
draft cards   go to prison
we are all assigned men who conscientiously object
to everything
but peace

I thought my war was over
all my patient marching
my strong left hand writing slogans on flags
to carry on my strong left shoulder

I thought my war was over
when my friend with one leg blown away
in war blew his brains out carefully in his garage
his strong right hand holding the gun

I thought my war was over
when I stopped writing poems
about nixon and god and babies burning

I was wrong
today all this week all last week
the war comes back
I was wrong because my son says
"today I met a man who writes about vietnam.
was that your war, mom?"
I was wrong because my son says
"here's a picture in the paper of that man.
does he say the words of war in his story?"
I answer and realize my son wants to share my war
until he gets one
of his own

we are all assigned children to love
they may not come from our bodies   that hardly matters
but we all must claim children to love
we are all assigned children to learn from
to teach the wearying truths of war to

we are all assigned a war and I have mine
I must not forget
that the title of this poem is a lie
there will never be any way for me to know
that the war is over

Dialogue

I ask my mother to remember
the tennis courts   nets always
too high or sagging like old ones in the park

I asked my father about the sun
breaking on our backs as we struggled
to bring order to the wild raspberry patch

I asked a stranger on a country street
about orion's belt   about his dagger
about winter's secret constellations

I asked my lover to notice the light
how it fills all second story windows   fills steeples
fills the white car at quarter to five in a winter afternoon

my mother takes that single memory
turns it to a recital of my childhood
clarified through the sieve of her watching eyes

my father   gone now and cold
answered   keep working
summer is brief here

the stranger said only that he liked stars
too shy to say more
an innocent in a world of dark

my lover listened said the light was Italian
had traveled here from Florence   said the light
was correct   that twilight was good
said he would not leave in twilight in winter in that light

there have been questions
I never knew there were answers to

there have been so many answers
they have all been right